Journey

Expressions of the I Ching

Journey

Expressions of the I Ching

Nancy Parker

Ashland Hills Press

Copyright 2015 by Nancy A. Parker. All rights reserved.

No part of this book may be reproduced or transmitted in any form or by any means, electronic or mechanical, including photocopying or recording, or by any information storage and retrieval system, without written permission from the author, except for brief quotations embodied in critical articles and reviews. For information, contact the publisher.

Cover photo "Caribou Lake," by Nancy Parker.

ISBN 978-0-9642272-8-6

Library of Congress Control Number: 2015903948

Published by Ashland Hills Press, P.O. Box 992, Ashland, OR 97520
Phone 541-951-1129

First Edition.

To my family.

Introduction

Nine years ago, I began this *Journey* as a means to approach the *I Ching* from both a spiritual and literary perspective. The project grew out of an earlier effort to depict in graphic form the sixty-four amino acid triplet sequences in DNA. The number sixty-four emerges in both our DNA and in the *I Ching* as significant, mathematically, biologically and by extension, spiritually. With this project, I wished to create a statement about each of the sixty-four *I Ching* hexagrams in a six-line word shape to match its broken line / single-line, *yin/yang* structure.

My approach to this project was also strongly influenced by my love for hiking and backpacking and my experiences being outdoors in wild, isolated places for extended periods of time. I have found in distance hiking a strong parallel to life's journey including it tremendous challenges and difficulties as well as its exuberant highs. Many of the expressions in this book reflect metaphorically these outdoor experiences. In addition, the influence of my decades-long study of *A Course in Miracles* is evident in this work.

For each expression, I began by meditating on the traditional meaning of the hexagram. I then begin to write in more or less a stream-of-consciousness manner but imposing on the process an overlaying discipline—to fit the words into the hexagram's actual physical shape. At any given moment, I might have produced a different expression, so each one is but a snapshot. At first, I referred to each as a poem, but that idea quickly came to seem both burdensome and daunting. Some expressions may seem poetic while others are more prescriptive. Once I had unloaded the burden of having to produce fine poetry, the expressions flowed more freely; I simply allowed to come whatever came.

The first few dozen expressions were completed in 2005. After that, I worked sporadically. In the last half of 2014, my life path took on some twists and turns that spurred me to delve more deeply and substantively into the *I Ching*, and, at the same time, complete this work. In the process, I have learned a great deal about the essence of this ancient "binary" philosophy; in many of the hexagrams' meanings, I recognized their implicit opposites.

With that recognition came an understanding that, as humans embodying universal energy, we enfold these dualities and, for the most part, do not express one side of each without also having understood and experienced the other. In this I found an enduring lesson—that, as expressed in the Hindu religion, *tat twan asi*, "I am that too." I am all these experiences and expressions, the so-called positive as well as negative, which makes me altogether human. To live what *I Ching* sages refer to as a "superior life," I am meant to come to an acceptance of all facets of myself and, by extension, everyone else. With an understanding that my thoughts manifest, this project has cracked open my heart into a deeper compassion and brought me to a more profound sense of what it is to be human. I have also taken in more deeply a recognition of the energetic impact and manifestation of my own thoughts.

Each of the hexagram expressions comprises a single page. On the facing page for each I have added the Chinese symbol that I found most apt for the meaning of the hexagram. Beneath that, I have left a space headed "Reflections," a place for you, the reader, to create your own expressions and/or note down your thoughts. This is also a workbook/journal. I encourage you to create your own expressions and would love to hear from you about them and about your process.

A Brief *I Ching* History

The brief overview that follows is in no way intended as a comprehensive review or explanation of the *I Ching* or the divination process. That is not my intention in this book. Nor is *Journey, Expressions of the I Ching* meant to be in any way a conclusive compilation of *I Ching* wisdom.

According to legend, the *I Ching* (pronounced *Yee Jing*) or Book of Changes, was created by a Chinese sage named *Fu Hsi* at some point in history prior to around 3000 BC, the time when writing first began in ancient China. The *I Ching* and its teachings were, by 3000 BC, already part of the oral tradition. Once written down, the philosophy spread and flourished.

Toward the end of the *Shang* Dynasty (1766-1121 BC), a learned *I Ching* scholar named *Wen* was imprisoned for opposing the tyrannical emperor, *Chou Shin*. While incarcerated, *Wen* relied on the great wisdom of the *I Ching* to keep himself alive, and he also further interpreted *I Ching* teachings and rearranged the sequence of the hexagrams, or *kua*, into their present order. Inspired by his father's work, *Wen's* son, *Yu*, overthrew the tyrannical emperor *Chou Shin* and went on to establish a lineage of leadership in China that relied on *I Ching* teachings and lasted over 800 years.

In 551 BC, the great scholar and sage Confucius is known to have begun studying the *I Ching*. Toward the end of his life, he is believed to have remarked that, "If some years could be added to my life, I would give fifty of them to the study of the *I Ching* and might then avoid falling into great error."

The ancient wisdom of the *I Ching* has been handed down over these past several millennia to modern times, making it the oldest known philosophy in all of human history.

A Binary System of Divination

The *I Ching* is a binary system, not unlike the binary numeric system consisting of ones and zeroes. The *I Ching* has been used to divine the answers to life questions. To use the system, one considers a question or issue of concern in one's life. One meditates upon the issue, considering all aspects and exploring one's feelings and energy associated with the issue. While doing this, one throws a set of coins, recording the heads-or-tails results as either a broken line *(yin)* or a solid line *(yang)*, for each of six tosses, and marking down results by stacking these broken or solid lines one upon the other until a "hexagram" of six lines is created. One then looks up the hexagram and consults the corresponding *I Ching* teaching.

In ancient times, divining was performed by casting yarrow sticks or by reading lines in tortoise shells. For obvious reasons and thankfully so, the tortoise shell method is no longer used. Regardless of the method, it is the formulation of the question coupled with meditation upon that question that infuses the process with energy, or *chi*. It is understood today that our thoughts and energy do measurably manifest; at the quantum level, for example, the intention and/or expectation of an experimenter influence the outcome of a quantum experiment. Realizing that our thoughts are themselves energy having real and significant consequence, we can use whichever *I Ching* divining method we wish to bring to the surface answers to life questions which actually already exist within our higher knowing selves.

Forming a Question

The question you focus upon should not be a yes/no question. Try asking instead, "What if I...," or "How can I...?" or "What is the best approach or attitude I can bring to this situation?" You might ask, "What effect would it bring to bear on the situation if I did x, y, or z?" An open-ended question such as, "What do I need to know about this situation?" is also a good approach. Notice that none of these question formulations asks, either in spirit or substance, "What is going to happen?" Nor does one effectively ask, "Does so-and-so love me?" While it is a binary system, the *I Ching* is not likely to yield meaningful answers to such questions. Instead of asking whether so-and-so loves me, you might ask, "What do I need to know about my relationship with so-and-so?"

The Three-Coin Method

Gather three coins with distinct head/tail sides. Focusing deeply on your question, cast the coins onto a flat surface. Your results will be one of four patterns:

Three tails	"Changing *Yin*,"	------- -------
Two tails, one head	"*Yang*"	------------------
One tail, two heads	"*Yin*"	------- -------
Three heads	"Changing *Yang*"	------------------

I will explain the "changing" *yin* and *yang* lines in a moment. First, continuing to focus on your question, repeat the casting of the three coins six times and record each toss, starting at the bottom and stacking each solid or broken line, one atop the other, noting where any "changing" lines occur. The result is your "primary hexagram," and you now look up the reading corresponding with this hexagram. This is the central key to your answer, the setting that defines what can or will unfold regarding your question.

Most castings contain one or more "changing lines," i.e., lines formed by tossing either three heads or three tails; and their presence in a reading adds new meaning and dimension. Once you've identified your primary hexagram, re-do your lines, with the changing lines marked as their opposite—if the line is broken (or *yin*), change it to unbroken (or *yang*); and if the line is unbroken, change it to broken. When every changing line has been transformed to its opposite, the resulting hexagram is your "relating hexagram."

Countless tomes have been written exploring the interaction and relationship of the primary hexagram to the relating hexagram. Exactly what the relating hexagram means for you depends on the sort of question you pose as well as how the two hexagrams' meanings relate to each other. The relating hexagram is considered more subjective and may function as the direction or pull on the situation of the primary hexagram. Or it could simply augment the primary hexagram's teaching.

For example, consider your coin toss yields Hexagram 21, Biting Through, Problem-Solving, and that line two is "Changing Yin":

Primary Hexagram 21:   Relating Hexagram 38:
-----------------   -----------------
------- -------   ------- -------
-----------------   -----------------
------- -------   ------- -------
------- ------- Changing Yin→   ----------------- Yang
-----------------   -----------------

The relating Hexagram is 38, Opposition, Mirroring. You would read this hexagram to supplement the meaning of Hexagram 21 regarding your question.

Finally, at the end of this book, I have included an index. It provides an alphabetized list of traits, characteristics, actions, aspects and emotions indexed to their relevant hexagrams. Use this if, for example, you have identified an emotional condition you are experiencing and wish to find relevant teachings without using a divining method.

My thanks go to friends who encouraged me along the way as I worked on this book. Specifically I wish to thank Jody and Dave Hodges who, early on, took up this work, even in its unfinished state, in connection with their *chi gong* energy work and practice. However you choose to use this book, I hope you find it enriches your life and augments your own *Journey*.

The Sixty-Four Hexagrams of the I Ching

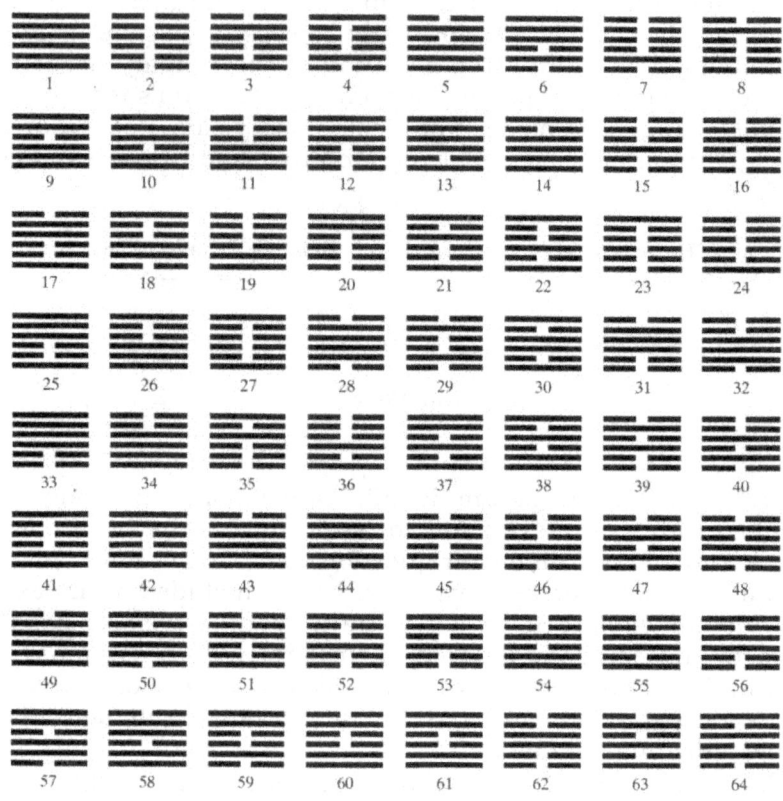

1 – The Creative

"CH'IEN"

CH'IEN - Yang, spirit power, creative and destructive; unceasing forward motion, dynamic, enduring, untiring; firm, stable; heaven, sovereign, father.

The idea arrives, a deeply mysterious gift wrapped in choice: to accept or release it; it entices me—the energy, the pull of it, appearing in such an offhanded way, as raindrops tapping lightly, leaves drifting down, settling softly, a quiet invitation.

"Yang"

Reflections

_____

_____

_____

_____

_____

_____

_____

_____

2 – The Receptive

"K'UN"

*K'UN - Yin - surface of the world; concrete extension;
basis of all existence where CH'IEN exerts
its power; an all-involving service;
earth; Moon, wife, mother.*

Take in the idea: a journey exploring
inner and outer   landscapes, a waxing
moon as guide,   we are led wisely, for
clearly we belong   to this temporal axis,
denizens of this   third planet from our
star, we travel on, safe on mother earth.

"Yin"

Reflections

_____

_____

_____

_____

_____

_____

_____

_____

3 – Difficulty at the Beginning

"CHUN"

CHUN - Begin or cause to grow; assemble, accumulate, bring under control; hoard possessions; establish a military camp; difficult, arduous.

Setting out, I have left behind much that's easy and familiar; I harbor doubts and wonder whether I will find the way; but the way immediately ahead of me is clear; if all paths finally lead one home, then my destination is inevitable; a journey begins with a single step and then another.

"Difficulty"

Reflections

_____
_____
_____
_____
_____
_____
_____
_____
_____
_____

4 – Youthful Folly Masking, Educating

"MENG"

MENG - To cover, pull over, hide, conceal; a lid or cover; clouded awareness, ignorance, immaturity; unseen beginnings.

An impenetrable fog has settled over the trail,
I cannot remember at all how this path
appeared before it was obscured to me;
I pause, take a few long, deep breaths;
you go on ahead, I'll catch up; I cannot walk
this path with you 'til my fog has lifted.

"Immature"

Reflections

_____
_____
_____
_____
_____
_____
_____
_____

5 – Waiting, Nourishment, Serving

"HSU"

*HSU - To take care of, look out for, serve;
turn your mind to what is necessary;
to wait or wait upon; to hesitate.*

There are times when all the obvious answers seem to be a non-answers, when the wisest course of action is no action; at such times, it is best if I do not forge ahead. Instead, I would do well to nurture and attend to others, look after them and trust: answers may arise from within a quiet mind.

"Wating"

Reflections

_____
_____
_____
_____
_____
_____
_____
_____

6 – Conflict, Compromising

"SUNG"

*SUNG - Disputation, to plead in court,
to contend before a ruler; to demand justice;
wrangles, quarrels, litigation.*

You are wrong, and I am right. I have seen the light whereas you see only darkness. Hear me out, I insist. But wait—beside my precipice of obstinate certainty & yours there exists a common ground of understanding. On three , let us each take one step away from the edge: One......two......three.

"Conflict"

Reflections

7 – The Army

"SHIH"

SHIH - Troops; an organized unit, a metropolis; leader, general, model, master; to organize, make functional; to take as a model, imitate.

Did you both explore each and every option?
sit down and talk till you were out of words?
consider the dire cost in blood and treasure?
envision survivors' grief, the orphaned children?
Remember history? Wars are based on
lies we tell ourselves about what is possible.

"Fighter"

Reflections

8 – Holding Together, Uniting

"PI"

PI - To order things and put them in classes; to compare and select; to discover what you belong with; to select and harmonize, unite.

When I contemplate our disconnected lives,
the minutia that seems true enough to break us,
then I *re*learn—for I have learned this more
than once—that sep-aration is illusion, and
in that remembrance our seeming brokenness
is mended; you and I—two sides, one coin.

"Uniting"

Reflections

_____
_____
_____
_____
_____
_____
_____
_____
_____

9 – Taming Power of the Small, Small Gains

"HSIAO CH'U"

HSIAO: Little, common, unimportant; adapting to whatever crosses your path; ability to move in harmonious relation to the vicissitudes of life.

CH'U: To hoard, gather, retain, herd together; domesticate, tame.

Today I shall mend clothes and rake the leaves, sew on buttons, sweep and dust, do laundry; I give myself to these ordinary tasks, attend to them with mindfulness; next thing I know, the extraordinary tasks, the ones I most resisted, are managed almost without effort.

"Unimportant"

Reflections

_____
_____
_____
_____
_____
_____
_____
_____
_____

10 – Treading the Path

"LU"

*Steps, path, track; footsteps; to walk a path or way;
the course of stars; to act, practice, conduct;
means of subsistence.*

I walk the paths of stars in the orbital plane of my planet, find grandeur and amazement in every individual small step, each revealing its own inhabitants of the ink black sky: look there—Orion's belt and sword, Arcturas, Southern Cross; gnarled rock beneath my feet.

"Walking"

Reflections

_____
_____
_____
_____
_____
_____
_____
_____

11 – Peace, Harmonizing, Balancing

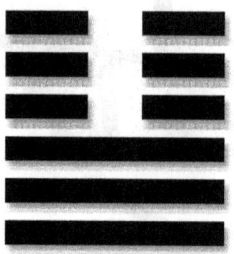

"T'AI"

*To spread and reach everywhere, permeate, diffuse;
To communicate; great, extensive, abundant,
prosperous, smooth, slippery; extreme, extravagant,
prodigal. Mt. T'ai in Eastern China was a sacred
mountain connecting heaven and Earth to which the
emperor made offerings to establish
harmony between humans and the great spirits.*

The granite rock shelf slopes into Caribou Lake; I rest there and watch the reflections of sky and encircling peaks; this lake is more like home to me than any other place; its constant resident is peace, and I come here in my dreams whenever I feel the world is lost to me.

"Peace"

Reflections

12 – Standstill, Stagnation

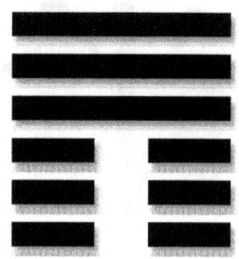

"PI"

Closed, stopped; to bar the way; an obstacle; unfortunate, wicked; to refuse, disapprove, deny. blocked communication.

Why did I not call out to you? What prevented me? Stubborn pride? Self-righteousness? False piety? These small solemn judgments laid as wreaths on tombs, burying in stone your truth and then of course my own; for now I clearly see: I cannot entomb you except by burying me.

"Stagnation"

Reflections

___
___
___
___
___
___
___
___
___

13 – Fellowship

"T'UNG JEN"

T'UNG: To harmonize, unite, equalize, assemble, agree; to be together at once, same time and place.

JEN: Humans individually and collectively; humankind.

What were the chances that, of all the lives lived, and all that ever will be lived, and all the times, those passed and yet to come, and of all the places on planets orbiting stars, in galaxies spiraling across the universe,   what were the chances it would be only you and I, here, now, together?

"Fellowship"

Reflections

14 – Possession in Great Measure

"TA YU"

TA: big, noble, important, very; to orient the will toward a self-imposed goal, to impose direction; the ability to lead or guide your life.

YU: to be in possession of, to have or own; possessions.

The universe is the masterpiece of transformation: matter is constantly reconstituted, recycled, reformed; even my physical form is remade daily; in the universe of form, nothing is truly our own; at most, we are custodians, caretakers of stardust; we possess nothing, everything, infinitely abundant.

"Prosperity"

Reflections

_____

_____

_____

_____

_____

_____

_____

_____

15 – Modesty

"CH'IEN"

CH'IEN - To think and speak of oneself in a modest way; respectful, unassuming, retiring, unobtrusive; yielding, compliant, reverent, humble.

Each and every ordinary one of us
is extraordinarily endowed; humility
flows from that truth; I recognize
the grandeur of my brother; take in his words
for he has dwelt in many realms,
lived many births died many deaths.

"Modesty"

Reflections

_____

_____

_____

_____

_____

_____

_____

_____

16 – Enthusiasm, Foresight, Preparing

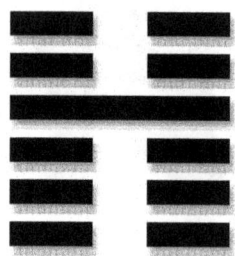

"YU"

YU - Ready, prepared for, to prearrange, take precaution, think beforehand; satisfied, at ease.

Most mornings upon awakening
I spend some time imagining my day,
visualizing the possibility and considering
how this fine day might well be lived;
each day is a lifetime: I am born
each morning, and die each night.

"Preparing"

Reflections

___
___
___
___
___
___
___
___
___

17 – Following, Believing

"SUI"

SUI - To come or go after, to pursue; impelled to move; come after in inevitable sequence; move in the same direction; comply with whatever is ahead; to follow a way or religion; according to, next, subsequent.

Does it matter whether I steadfastly adhere
to anyone else's stone-carved articles of faith?
I am compelled onward by the energy of my life,
and with or with- out a creed, the
destination is illusion, now is all we have,
today's starting point in the ongoing journey.

"Adhering"

Reflections

18 – Correcting, Working on What Has Been Spoiled

"KU"

KU - Rotting, poisonous; intestinal worms, venomous insects, evil magic; disorder, error; to pervert by seduction or flattery; an unquiet ghost.

I learned it is up to me to clean up my messes, not a bad prescription for some of the world's woes; if each practiced that, we might honor more, destroy less, cherish dearly, spill and spoil less, tread more lightly, leaving fewer footprints behind, fewer unquiet ghosts of rampage.

"Correction"

Reflections

_____
_____
_____
_____
_____
_____
_____
_____
_____

19 – Approaching with Deference

"LIN"

LIN - To approach, to behold with care, to look down on sympathetically, to condescend; to bless or curse by coming nearer; a superior visiting an inferior.

I came upon a waterfall unexpectedly one day while hiking, a mighty, foaming, coursing burst of energy splitting rock, cascading downward, spewing spray into a rainbow aura; the air pulsed its power, resonated grace; I bowed my head, breathed it in, and felt blessed.

"Homage"

Reflections

_____
_____
_____
_____
_____
_____
_____
_____
_____

20 – Admiring, Contemplation of a View

"KUAN"

KUAN - To contemplate, observe from a distance; to look at carefully, to gaze at; also, a monastery, an observatory; to divine through liquid in a cup.

Millions of years ago, a star was born in a distant nebula; today I view that birth through Hubble's eyes, see its history unfolding and wonder: what became of that nascent star? Has it mothered planets, cradled life that even now stands gazing at my Sun in wonder?

"Admiring"

Reflections

_____
_____
_____
_____
_____
_____
_____
_____
_____

21 – Biting Through, Problem-Solving

"SHIH HO"

SHIH: to bite away, chew; to bite persistently and remove; To snap at, nibble; to reach the essential by removing the unnecessary.

HO: to close the jaws, bite through, crush between teeth.

Viewed one way, there are no problems, only
a resistance; my   misperception of a
problem arises from non-acceptance of reality;
from my especially   beveled gaze I know
a single measure   of a vast symphony,
and then I imagine I have understood it all.

"Bite through"

Reflections

22 – Grace, Adorning

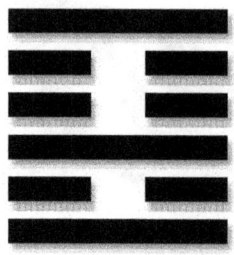

"PI"

PI - To embellish, ornament, deck out, beautify; variegated flowers; elegant, brilliant; also energetic, passionate, eager, intrepid, capable of great effort; brave.

Spring brings on an exuberant public show, gardens of crocuses, tulips and daffodils for all to see; one day, alone in a hidden canyon, I came upon a wild mountain dogwood in stunning bloom, graceful, white amid the dark slopes of pine and fir, for my eyes, no one else's—profligate spring.

"Embellish"

Reflections

_____
_____
_____
_____
_____
_____
_____
_____

23 - Splitting Apart, Pruning, Cutting Back

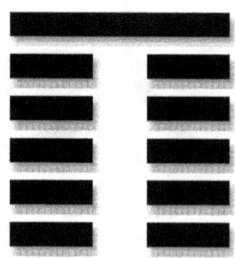

"PO"

PO - To flay, peel skin; remove, uncover, degrade, split, slice; reduce to essentials; slaughter an animal.

Let go of every single thing that is untrue:
all matters that no longer serve,
all treasured hurts withered fictions;
beneath these now- healed wounds—
new skin; I open to whatever truth
now seeks to enter this green heart.

"Cutting back"

Reflections

_____
_____
_____
_____
_____
_____
_____
_____
_____

24 - Return, the Turning Point

"FU"

FU - Go back, turn back to the starting point; recur, reappear, come again; restore, recover, retrace; return to an earlier time or place.

There is no harm in doubling back
recognizing error choosing another
way; better than clinging to a path
that leads away from what is true;
first one ought to accept that one is
human, fallible; therein stirs perfection.

"Restore, return"

Reflections

_____

_____

_____

_____

_____

_____

_____

_____

_____

25 - The Unexpected, Innocence, Disentangling

"WU WANG"

WU - devoid of

WANG - caught up in, entangled; disorder, incoherence, wild, vain, idle, futile, reckless.

The ego has a most compelling agenda and definite opinions on how everyone and everything ought to be; locked in ego, I am unnerved by any deviation from this tidy scheme; energy devoured by my resistance, I suffer 'til I finally drop all expectations and make peace with all, exactly as it is.

"Innocence"

Reflections

_____
_____
_____
_____
_____
_____
_____
_____
_____

26 - The Taming Power of the Great Holding Firm

"TA CH'U"

TA - Big, noble, important, to orient the will toward a self-imposed goal, impose direction; ability to lead or guide your life.

CH'U - to hoard, gather, retain, herd together; control, restrain; domesticate, tame, feed, sustain.

Settle the mastermind with conviction upon a goal, gather all resources toward that noble end; choose the path that best will lead one there; visualize the ultimate outcome in minute detail, give to this effort your full and loving attention and tame all lurking fears of failure and success.

"Tame"

Reflections

_____

_____

_____

_____

_____

_____

_____

_____

_____

27 - The Corners of the Mouth, Providing Nourishment, Hungering

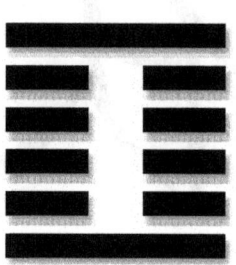

"YI"

Mouth, jaws, cheeks, chin; to take in, ingest; to feed, nourish, sustain, rear; furnish what is necessary.

There are as many kinds of hunger as there are nourishments; food is only one of them; mystics fast both to know hunger's force and discover spirit's great surfeit; I ingest food mindfully, for I see that I feed both body and spirit; the two are one within me.

"Ingest"

Reflections

_____
_____
_____
_____
_____
_____
_____
_____
_____

28 - Preponderance of the Great Exceeding

"TA KUO"

TA - Big, noble, important, to orient the will toward a self-imposed goal, impose direction; ability to lead or guide your life.

KUO - To go beyond, pass by, pass over; excessive; transgress, error, fault.

My carefully drawn design looked so fine on paper, how could it not succeed? Before the ink is slightly dry, before a word is read I begin to celebrate, lean as if to take a bow; hold on, my dear, your design is flawed, its purpose is not clear; begin again, revise.

"Flaw"

Reflections

_____
_____
_____
_____
_____
_____
_____
_____
_____

29 - The Abysmal, Water, Containing, Control

"HSI K'AN"

HSI - Practice, rehearse, train, coach; again and again; familiar with, skilled; repeat a lesson, drive, impulse.

K'AN - Dangerous place; a hole, cavity, hollow; pit, snare, trap, grave, precipice; critical time, test, risky.

Whenever we choose to become ensnared in the trap of denial as to who we really are, we lose our way; in consciousness we are beloved beyond limit and gifted beyond all measure, treasured beings each with a vital role to play in the vastness of creation; and so, right now, choose freedom.

"Trap"

Reflections

30 - The Clinging, Fire Guiding

"LI"

LI - Glowing light, spreading in all directions; light-giving, discriminating, articulating; divide and arrange in order; the power of consciousness.

Illumination defines the sharp edges of matter, distills all consciousness, defines the shape and form of all I see, without light, I do not exist, I have no form, no being, and with the light I am everything—oneness made whole.

"Consciousness"

Reflections

31 - Influence, Wooing, Restrained Joining

"HSIEN"

HSIEN - To come into contact with, influence; to reach, join together; to put together; put together as parts of a previously separated whole; to come into conjunction, as the celestial bodies; totally, completely.

For a time I believed that you and I were broken, imagined I had injured you, or vice versa, thought we'd never heal our separate broken hearts; but separation is an illusion created by fear and mended in an instant; I reach 'cross the rift and take your hand.

"Join Together"

Reflections

_____
_____
_____
_____
_____
_____
_____
_____
_____

32 - Duration, Committing

"HENG"

HENG - To continue in the same way and spirit; constant, perpetual, regular; self-renewing; extend everywhere; the moon almost full.

Someone asked me, "Are you sure you are on the right path?" I said I believe I am; Someone said, "It looks all wrong to me, the way you go," and I replied, "I believe it is the path I am to take," and continued on my way; my doubts reflected, my certainty replied.

"Enduring"

Reflections

33 - Retreat, Withdraw

"TUN"

TUN - To withdraw, run away, flee; conceal yourself, become obscure, invisible; secluded, non-social.

At times, I choose to close myself within a vault of heavy steel and remove my awareness from everyone and everything that is outside; I listen instead to whatever is within, until I reach a sense of no thing; in that spaciousness I finally am renewed and unlock the door.

"Withdraw"

Reflections

_____

_____

_____

_____

_____

_____

_____

_____

_____

34 - The Power of the Great Inspiring

"TA CHUANG"

TA - Big, noble, important, to orient the will toward a self-imposed goal, impose direction; ability to lead or guide your life.

CHUANG - Inspire, animate; strong, robust; full-grown, flourishing, abundant; damage through unrestrained strength.

Teachers of wisdom have offered me their road maps leading home; some of them were humble, respectful of my path and way, others required that I worship for their truth; in the end, the truest home I ever found was the one here, within my quiet listening heart.

Inspire"

Reflections

_____
_____
_____
_____
_____
_____
_____
_____

35 - Progress, Progressing

"CHIN"

CHIN - To grow and flourish, as young plants in the sun; to increase, progress, permeate, impregnate; attached to.

There is seasonal rhythm to my growth,
like breathing out   and breathing in,
the tides, the moon, both wax and wane;
celebrate the yin,   revel in the yang,
each one relying   on the other's *chi;*
make peace with   ev'ry pulsing beat.

"Progress"

Reflections

_____

_____

_____

_____

_____

_____

_____

_____

36 - Darkening of the Light

"MING YI"

MING - Light-giving aspect of burning; heavenly bodies and consciousness; with fire, the symbol of the trigram radiance.

YI - To keep out of sight, remote, distant from the center; to equalize by lowering; to squat, level, make ordinary; pacified, colorless; to cut, wound, destroy.

I am reserving my energy, gathering it, holding it close; like water pressure: if bled off in small amounts, the forceful flow becomes a trickle; and so there is a time to harbor and harness one's *chi*, that it may build and burst upon the world.

"Darken"

Reflections

37 - The Family, Clan

"CHIA JEN"

CHIA - Home, house, household, family; domestic, within doors; to live inside.

JEN - Humans individually and collectively, humankind.

My dog, my family, my pals, the people of my town, of my county, my state, my countrymen, western hemispherians, each & every single earthling. solar systemians, Alpha Centaurians, beings of the Milky Way Galaxy, all beings of this universe, and of this multiverse—you are each and all my clan.

"Family"

Reflections

_____

_____

_____

_____

_____

_____

_____

_____

_____

38 - Opposition, Mirroring

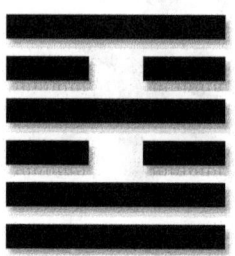

"K'UEI"

K'UEI - Separate, opposing; contrary, mutually exclusive; distant from, absent, remote; animosity, anger; astronomical or polar opposition.

I'll never see myself as you perceive me, who I see is an opposite reflection, scars and quirks and smiles in reverse; do others see us truer than we see ourselves? Light reflected is still light, and all the light is ultimately reflected.

"Face to face"

Reflections

_____
_____
_____
_____
_____
_____
_____
_____

39 - Obstruction, Bypassing

"CHIEN"

CHIEN - To walk lamely, proceed haltingly; weak-legged, afflicted, crooked, feeble, weak; unfortunate, difficult.

One hot afternoon along a treeless track
I came apart, could not take another step,
the relentless sun beat down, dried out
my tears and sweat; I stood bent over, spent,
then took one step and then one more
until I came upon the shelter of a tree.

"Obstruction"

Reflections

___
___
___
___
___
___
___
___
___

40 - Deliverance

"HSIEH"

HSIEH - To loosen, disjoin, untie, sever, scatter, analyze, explain, understand; to release, dispel sorrow; eliminate effects, solve problems; resolution, deliverance.

I rested there beneath the shading tree, drew water from a spring nearby and washed away the salt of sweat and tears; henceforth I must remember this: when spent, bent over and hopeless, take just one step and then another.

"Relief"

Reflections

_____

_____

_____

_____

_____

_____

_____

_____

_____

41 - Reduce, Decrease or Concentrate

"SUN"

SUN - To lessen, make smaller; take away from; to lose, damage, spoil, wound; bad luck, blame, criticize; to offer up or give away.

Indeed, this has been a difficult and trying time: wars, illness, poverty despair, malfeasance, incompetence among those we chose to lead, betrayed by some we loved and trusted; so now it may be time to withdraw focus from all of that and turn instead within, where wholeness is.

"Misfortune"

Reflections

_____
_____
_____
_____
_____
_____
_____
_____
_____

42 - Increase, Augmenting, Ascending

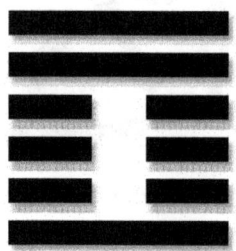

"YI"

YI - To increase, advance, promote, benefit, strengthen; pour in more; full, superabundant; restorative.

Winter grabbed hold of Fall as if to not let go, encased the rusted leaves in frost; how can I remember clearly the color of green when all is draped in gray? But soon: crocuses everywhere! tulips and daffodils! new leaves! Resilient Spring reclaims her ken.

"Strengthen"

Reflections

_____
_____
_____
_____
_____
_____
_____
_____
_____

43 - Breakthrough, Seedlings, Cuttings, Spread Out

"KUAI"

*KUAI - To separate, fork, cut off, decide;
to pull or flow in different directions;
certain, settled; prompt, decisive, stern.*

The path is forked   I must decide now to turn left or to go right; I cannot do both; the two directions call to me, but I can only take one. At the fork, I sit awhile, listen to my heart, consult energy, feel each option, then rise and choose: what is there to lose?

"Choose"

Reflections

44 - Coming to Meet, Persuading, Seducing

"KOU"

KOU - Intense, driven encounter, at once transitory and enduring as the reflection of primal yin and yang; to meet, encounter, copulate; mating animals; magnetism, gravity; to be gripped by impersonal forces.

We take each other in, hold each other close, both incapable of resisting this primal urge; demolishing reticence, we set aside mistrust, seducing one another, our barriers recede, we become as one and, in the joining, reclaim the realization: you and I   we were always one.

"Mating"

Reflections

45 - Gathering Together

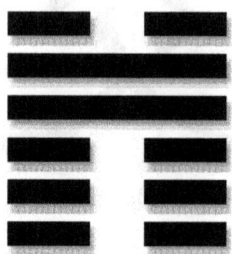

"TS'UI"

TS'UI - To pack together; tight groups of people, animals, or things; to collect, gather, assemble, concentrate; a bunch, crowd, collection.

When life splinters apart, and disparate elements are flung wide and far, my aloneness can convince me I have erred; I must stop then, create a gathering of the ones I love, bring them all here, hold them all close, make a celebration till splinters mend.

"Crowd"

Reflections

_____
_____
_____
_____
_____
_____
_____
_____

46 - Pushing Upward, Rising

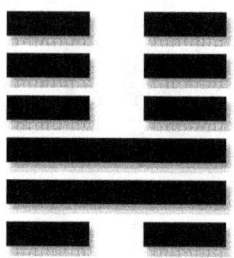

"SHENG"

SHENG - To go up, to climb step by step, to rise in office; to advance through effort; to bring out and fulfill; ascension through distillation.

The next part of the trail is so steep,
the load I carry is far too much to bear;
I step off the path, unshoulder my pack,
sift through it all and keep only what I need;
leaving the rest behind, I then take up my
pack and climb up and climb, and up.

"Rising"

Reflections

_____
_____
_____
_____
_____
_____
_____
_____
_____

47 - Oppression, Confinement

"K'UN"

K'UN - To enclose, restrict, limit; oppressed, impoverished; distressed, afflicted; exhausted, disheartened, weary.

The truest part of me, the spirit deep within, can never be oppressed, disheartened or enslaved; I have sometimes chosen my own imprisonment, and invited others to participate in the plot but if I convinced myself they also wrote the play I was deluding myself, projecting it on them.

"Oppression"

Reflections

_____
_____
_____
_____
_____
_____
_____
_____
_____

48 - The Well

"CHING"

CHING - A water well at the center of fields; the rise and flow of water in a well; the rise and surge from an inner source; the center of life.

I Ching, the "Book of Changes," life's water—boiling coursing shifting freezing melting falling flowing; ocean- river-stream-creek earth's capillary system and my lifeblood; within one drop, one single snowflake, lives *chi* enough to heal our hearts and steer the stars.

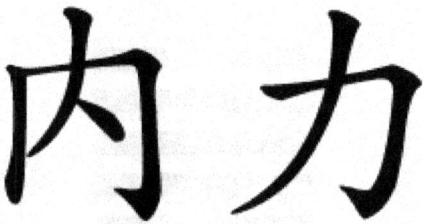

"Inner Strength"

Reflections

_____
_____
_____
_____
_____
_____
_____
_____
_____

49 - Revolution, Unmasking

"KO"

KO - To remove the covering, skin or hide; to change, renew or molt; to peel off; to revolt or overthrow from office.

Let me drop my veil, shuck off all adornment obscuring who I really am; uncovered I am vulnerable and feel afraid: what if you disapprove of what or who you see? Yet this is where real freedom can begin, for now you've seen me as I truly am and if you love me still, then there is nothing left for me to fear.

"Uncovering"

Reflections

___
___
___
___
___
___
___
___
___
___

50 - The Cauldron, Transforming

"TING"

TING - A melting or cooking pot, receptacle; to hold, contain, transform; secure; a sacred vessel used to cook food for sacrifice in honor of gods and ancestors.

If I would transform my present situation, I must throw into the pot all ingredients, both bitter and sweet, tart and tangy, loved and loathed, each element enfolded into the stew, accepting, honoring each—I am that too; the whole, greater than the sum of parts.

"Transforming"

Reflections

51 - The Arousing, Thunder, Enlightenment, Awareness

"CHEN"

CHEN - To arouse, excite, inspire; thunder rising from below; awe, alarm, trembling.

I was camped outside one night in thunder, lightning slashed the darkness, rain pounded down; afraid that night might be my last, I thought I'm much too small to play this large; when morning brought the sun and I'd survived, I took my greatest lesson from that violent night.

"Thunder"

Reflections

_____
_____
_____
_____
_____
_____
_____
_____
_____
_____

52. Keeping Still, the Mountain

"KEN"

KEN - A limit, boundary; to encounter an obstacle, to stop; to be still, quiet, motionless; to confine, enclose, mark off; turn around to look behind.

I have finally reached the top of the mountain, the one I have been climbing for so long, weary and elated, I decide to spend the night stretched out beneath the canopy of stars, rock, hard beneath me, air so thin, so high my lungs may burst, I rest, am still.

"Mountain"

Reflections

_____
_____
_____
_____
_____
_____
_____
_____

53 - Development, Gradual Progress

"CHIEN"

CHIEN - To advance incrementally; to penetrate deeply and surely, as water; stealthily; to mature; to permeate throughout; to influence.

At times, I walk so slowly that I feel no progress or motion at all—until I remember where I've been; then I clearly see I've come so far; the trail is downhill now and I am seasoned, but I have still a way to go; be mindful here, watch my footing lest I stumble off the trail.

"Gradual"

Reflections

_____
_____
_____
_____
_____
_____
_____
_____

54 - The Marrying Maiden

"KUEI MEI"

KUEI - To change to another form; persuade; to return to yourself or the place where you belong; restore, revert, become loyal; to give as a young girl in marriage.
MEI - A young girl, younger sister.

The young girl I was so many years ago was brave-hearted, incautious, sought adventure, was confident and bold; she lives on in me still and I sometimes call her forth, for hers is the energy that often moves me forward; it is to her I will one day return.

"Young girl"

Reflections

_____
_____
_____
_____
_____
_____
_____
_____
_____

55 - Abundance Overflowing

"FENG"

FENG - Abundant, plentiful; to become wealthy; exuberant, prolific; having many talents, property, friends; fullness, culmination; ripe, sumptuous.

Above a waterfall, I stop to watch it flow,
pools filling up with water, spilling over
tumbling down in rainbows of misting spray;
abundance is about flow; to join it, one must
enter the coursing river open-handed;
it does not flow through a fist that's clenched.

"Abundance"

Reflections

_____
_____
_____
_____
_____
_____
_____
_____
_____

56 - The Wanderer

"LU"

LU - To travel, stay in a place other than one's home; itinerant troops, temporary residents; visitor, guest, lodger.

Wandering without aim or purpose is not the way most are accustomed to moving in the world; wandering, I am in a mind state of nonattachment; that is not to say I am detached from or indifferent to the world but that I allow all that unfolds moment by moment to simply be as it is.

"Wanderer"

Reflections

57 - The Gentle Penetrating Wind

"SUN"

SUN - The base upon which things rest; support or foundation; mildly or subtly penetrating; nourishing; influencing.

The softest breeze touches my face, cools me, reassuring me I breathe the very breath of life; there is nothing here to fear, nothing from which to hide, no one who would impede the inevitable flow of abundant good; I live here, child of the universe at home in this realm.

"Gentle wind"

Reflections

_____
_____
_____
_____
_____
_____
_____
_____

58 - The Joyous Lake

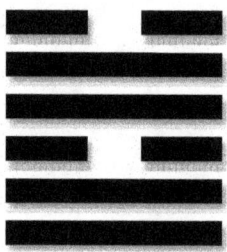

"TUI"

TUI - An open surface, a place where water accumulates; promoting interaction; responsive, free, unhindered; pleasing; an opening or passageway; to exchange or barter; straight or direct; self-reflecting.

Look into the water at stillness, reflecting back our faces against the sky; many come here, to drink it in, submerge themselves, be cleansed, or merely sit in the warm afternoon sun and ponder their journey; we are joined here, all of us, in a common purpose, each with a part to play.

"Lake"

Reflections

_____
_____
_____
_____
_____
_____
_____
_____

59 - Dispersion, Dissolution

"HUAN"

HUAN - To scatter, break up obstacles, illusions, fears or suspicions; to clear up misunderstandings; to disperse, dissolve, evaporate, disintegrate..

Today, a dense fog has lifted; all confusion and obstacles have dissolved; where once there was resistance, easy flow is restored; where I couldn't see the way ahead, the path is open to me; I go where the lights are green; let us walk this path together for a while.

"Dissolve"

Reflections

_____
_____
_____
_____
_____
_____
_____
_____
_____

60 - Limitation

"CHIEH"

CHIEH - To separate and distinguish; to join different things; to express thought through speech; joint, section, chapter, interval, unit of time; regulations; zodiac sign.

Are boundaries real? Fences imply they are; yet we move in a universe that is an infinite realm, dimensions fixed only by the reach of our conscious awareness; limitations as I perceive them could all be illusion, figments of an imagination that need only open wider to enfold the unbounded.

"Limitation"

Reflections

_____
_____
_____
_____
_____
_____
_____
_____
_____
_____

61 - Inner Truth

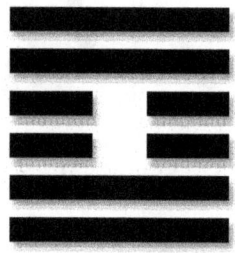

"CHUNG FU"

CHUNG - Inner, central; calm, stable; to place in the center; stable point that enables one to effectively deal with change.

FU - Accord between inner and outer in a particular moment; sincere, truthful, verified, reliable, in accord with the spirits.

Our thoughts are the same energy that fuels the universe, and they manifest in all we see and do; if you would change your experience, then change your thought; you are a magnificent creator—accept this as your natural power, claim it: you are the living energy embodiment of stars.

"Truth"

Reflections

_____
_____
_____
_____
_____
_____
_____
_____

62 - Preponderance of the Small

"HSIAO KUO"

HSIAO - Little, common, or unimportant; adapting to whatever crosses your path; ability to move in harmony with whatever comes along.

KUO - To go beyond or surpass, bypass, pass over.

Walking a section of trail strewn with rubble, I tread with focused care for every footfall; I am mindful of the impact of even small movements; if the energy of my every thought is manifest, then even the smallest of pebbles beneath my feet concerns me and lays claim to my attention.

"Unimportant"

Reflections

_____
_____
_____
_____
_____
_____
_____
_____
_____

63 - After Completion, Correct Sequence

"CHI CHI"

CHI - Completed, finished, has occurred.
CHI - To cross a river at a ford or shallow place; to overcome an obstacle, embark on a new course of action; to relieve.

I've finally reached the end of this long trail, and I've no idea what new trails may lie ahead; I feel a little sad but also jubilant; looking back on the rise and fall and turns the way I've come, I've taken this trail in to me and made it mine to guide me in whatever is to be my next journey.

"Sequence"

Reflections

_____
_____
_____
_____
_____
_____
_____
_____
_____

64 - Before Completion
Out of Sequence

"WEI CHI"

WEI - Temporal, negative; incomplete, has not occurred.
CHI - To cross a river at a ford or shallow place; to overcome an obstacle, embark on a new course of action; to relieve.

When a mutation occurs in our genetic sequence, it often brings about a great shift and an advancement for our species; we welcome such an unexpected rift, for it holds our potential growth within its asynchronous grasp; we must seize it, appreciate it: every thing changes.

"Out of order"

Reflections

Alphabetical Index to the 64 Hexagrams by Hexagram Number

A
Absent - 38
Abundant, abundance - 11, 14, 34, 42, 55
Accord - 61
Accumulate - 3
Adapt - 9
Adhere - 17
Admire - 20
Adorn, adornment - 22
Advance - 41, 46, 53
Afflicted, affliction - 39, 47
Agree, agreement - 13
Alarm - 51
Analyze - 40
Anger - 38
Animate - 34
Animosity - 38
Approach - 19
Arrange in order - 30
Arduous - 3
Army - 7
Arouse - 51
Ascend, ascending - 41, 46
Assemble - 3, 13, 45
Augment - 41
Awareness - 4, 51
Awe - 51

B
Balance, balancing - 11
Bar the way - 12
Barter - 58
Beautify, beauty - 22
Begin, beginning - 3
Behind - 52
Behold - 19
Believe, belief - 17

Beyond - 62
Biting through - 21
Blame - 41
Blocked - 12
Boundary - 52
Brave - 22
Break through - 43, 59
Brilliant - 22
Bunch - 45
Bypass - 39, 62

C
Cauldron - 50
Cavity - 29
Center - 48, 61
Change - 49, 50, 64
Chapter - 60
Chew - 21
Chi - 35, 36, 48
Clan - 37
Climb - 46
Cling - 30
Closed - 12
Clouded awareness - 4
Coach, teach - 29
Collect, collection - 45
Commit - 32
Common - 9, 62
Communicate - 11
Completion - 63, 64
Compromise - 6
Concentrate - 41, 45
Condescend - 19
Conflict - 6
Confine, confinement - 47, 52
Conscious, consciousness - 30, 36
Contain, container - 29, 50

Benefit - 42
Continue - 32
Control - 29
Copulate - 44
Contrary - 38
Correction - 18
Cover - 4
Creative - 1
Criticize - 41
Crowd - 45
Crush - 21
Cut back - 23

D
Damage - 41
Danger - 29
Darken - 36
Decisive - 43
Decrease - 41
Defer, deference - 19
Degrade - 23
Deliverance - 40
Deny - 12
Destroy, destructive - 1, 36, 41
Development - 53
Difficult, difficulty - 3, 9, 39
Direction - 14
Discriminate - 30
Disentangle - 25
Dishearten, disheartened - 47
Disintegrate - 58
Disorder - 18
Disperse - 58
Dispute - 6
Dissolution - 58
Distant - 20, 38
Divide - 30
Divine, divination - 20
Domesticate - 9, 26, 37
Duration - 32
Dynamic - 1

E
Eager - 22

Contemplate/tion - 20
Eat - 27
Educate - 4, 29
Ego - 4, 25
Embellish - 22
Enclose - 47, 52
End - 63
Enduring - 1
Energy - 1, 12, 22, 35, 36, 61
Enlighten, enlightenment - 51
Enthusiasm, enthusiastic - 16
Equalize - 13, 36
Error - 18
Evaporate - 59
Evil - 18
Excess, excessive - 28
Exchange - 58
Excite - 51
Exhausted - 47
Explain - 40
Extravagant - 11

F
Family - 37
Father - 1
Feed - 26, 27
Fellowship - 13
Finish - 63
Fire - 30, 36
Flatter, flattery - 18
Flourish - 34, 35
Flow - 48
Follow - 17
Folly - 4
Food - 27
Footsteps - 10
Fork (branch) - 43
Foresight - 16
Foundation - 57
Fulfill - 46
Fullness - 55
Futile, futility - 25

G
Gather - 8, 9, 26, 31, 45

Earth - 2
Gathering place - 58
Gaze - 20
General (military) - 7
Ghost - 18
Give away - 41
Glow - 30
Go back - 24
Goal - 14, 28
Grace - 22
Gradual - 53
Group together - 8, 9, 45
Guidance - 28

H
Harmonize - 8, 11, 13
Harmony - 62
Heaven, heavenly bodies - 1, 36
Herd together - 26
Hesitate - 5
Hide, hidden - 4, 36
Hoard, hoarding - 3, 26
Holding firm - 26
Holding together - 8
Home - 37
House - 37
Human, humankind - 13, 37
Humble, humility - 15
Hunger - 27

I
Idea - 1
Idle - 25
Ignorance, ignorant - 4
Illuminate - 30
Illusions - 59
Imitate - 7
Immature - 4
Important - 14
Impoverished - 47
Impregnate - 35
Incomplete - 64
Increase - 42
Inferior - 19
Influence - 31, 53

Inner truth - 61
Innocent, innocence - 25
Inspire, inspiration - 34, 51
Interactive - 58
Intrepid - 22
Invisible - 33
Itinerant - 56

J
Jaws - 21
Join - 31, 60
Journey - 2
Joyous - 58
Justice - 6

K

L
Lake - 58
Lame - 39
Lead, leader - 7
Learn - 29
Lesson - 29
Light - 30, 36
Limit, limitation - 47, 52, 60
Litigation - 6
Lodger - 56
Look down on - 19
Loosen - 40
Lose - 41
Loyal - 54
Luck, bad - 41

M
Magnetism - 44
Maiden - 54
Marry - 54
Mating - 44
Mature, maturing - 53
Meet, meeting - 44
Melt, melting - 50
Military - 7
Mirroring - 38
Misunderstanding - 58
Prepare - 16

Modesty - 15
Molt - 49
Monastery - 20
Moon - 2, 32
Mother - 2
Motionless - 52
Mountain - 52
Mouth - 27

N
Necessary - 5, 21, 27
Non-social - 33
Nourish, nourishment - 5, 27, 57
Nurture - 5

O
Observe, observatory - 20
Obstacle - 63, 64
Obstruct, obstruction - 39
Oppose, opposition - 38
Oppressed - 47
Organize - 7
Overcome - 28, 63
Overflow, overflowing - 55
Overthrow, overthrowing - 49
Ownership - 14

P
Passageway - 58
Passionate - 22
Path - 10, 43
Peace - 11
Peel, peel off - 23, 49
Penetrate - 53, 57
Permeate - 11, 35
Persuade, persuasive - 44, 54
Perversion - 18
Pit (hollow) - 29
Plead (in court) - 6
Plentiful - 55
Possession - 14
Practice - 10, 29
Precaution - 16
Robust - 34

Problem-solving - 21, 40
Progress - 35, 53
Property - 55
Prosper - 11
Prune (cut off) - 23
Push up - 46

Q
Quarrel - 6
Quiet - 18, 52

R
Radiant, radiance - 36
Reach - 31
Receptive - 2
Reckless - 25
Recover - 24
Reduce - 23, 41
Reflect, reflecting - 58
Refuse, refusal/ing - 12
Regulations - 60
Rejoin - 31
Reliable - 61
Relieve - 63
Religion - 17
Remote - 36
Repair - 31
Respect, respectful - 15
Resolute - 26
Resolution - 40
Resolve - 40
Responsive - 58
Restore - 24, 42, 54
Retrace (steps) - 24
Retreat - 24, 33
Restrict, restricting/ed - 47
Return - 24, 54
Reverent - 15
Revert - 54
Revolution - 49
Ripe - 55
Risk - 29
River (crossing) - 63, 64
Sustain - 26

Run away from - 33

S
Satisfied - 16
Scatter - 40
Secluded - 33
Seduce, seduction - 18, 44
Seeds, seedlings - 42
Self-reflecting - 58
Self-renew, self-renewing - 32
Separation - 8
Separate - 43
Sequence, sequential - 17, 63, 64
Service, serve - 2, 5
Sever - 40
Sincere - 61
Sister - 54
Slaughter - 23
Slice - 23
Small - 9, 62
Snare - 29
Solve - 40
Sovereign - 1
Speak - 60
Split apart - 23
Spread - 30, 32, 43
Spirit - 11, 32, 61
Spoil - 41
Stagnate, stagnation - 12
Standstill - 12
Stars - 10
Starting point - 24
Steps - 10
Still, stillness - 52
Stopped - 12
Strengthen - 42
Strong - 34
Subsistence - 10
Sumptuous - 55
Superior - 19
Support - 57
Surpass - 62

T
Talented - 55
Tame - 9, 26
Teach - 29
Temporal - 64
Test - 29
Thunder - 51
Time - 60, 64
Together - 13
Transcend - 28
Transform - 50
Trap - 29
Travel, traveler - 56
Treading (the path) - 10
Trivial - 9
Troops (military) - 7
Truth, truthful - 61
Turn around - 52
Turning point - 24

U
Ubiquitous - 11
Unassuming - 15
Uncover, uncovered - 49
Unexpected - 25
Unfortunate - 12, 39
Unimportant - 9, 62
Unmask, unmasked - 49
Unite, united, uniting - 8, 13
Unnecessary - 21
Unobtrusive - 15
Unquiet - 18
Unrestrained - 34
Untie, untied - 40

V
Verbalize - 60
Vessel - 50
Visitor - 56
Visualize - 16
Vocalize - 60

W

Wait, waiting - 5
Walk, walking - 10, 39
Wander, wanderer - 56
Way - 10, 12, 17, 32Weak - 39
Wealth, wealthy - 55
Weary - 47
Well (water) - 48
Wife - 2
Windy - 57
Withdraw - 33
Wound, wounded - 36, 41

X

Y
Yang - 1
Yielding - 15
Yin - 2, 15

Z
Zodiac - 60

www.ingramcontent.com/pod-product-compliance
Lightning Source LLC
Chambersburg PA
CBHW071119090426
42736CB00012B/1960